Puppets

Rebecca Quinn
Photography by Lyz Turner-Clark

CELEBRATION PRESS

Pearson Learning Group

Clean up!

When you see the words *Clean up!*, this means clean up any mess you have created. When you finish making your puppets, put away all your equipment and materials.

Contents

Fun With Finger Puppets

Finger puppets are easy to make and fun to play with—alone or with your friends. You can even write a short play and act it out using your puppets.

When you have made the puppets in this book, you can try making your own designs.

What sort of puppet would you like to make? A frog? A panda, a pig, or a parrot? For each puppet, follow the instructions and look carefully at the pictures for help.

Equipment

You will need this equipment for each puppet you make.

- scissors
- black felt pen
- white color pencil
- pencil
- craft glue

You will also need to use a template to make your puppets. A template is a shape that will help you make the puppet. The template is on page 7.

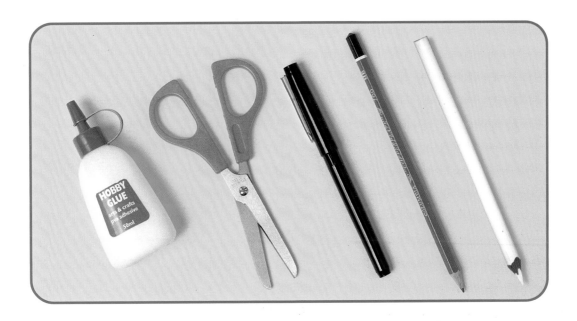

Materials

You will need these materials for each puppet you make.

- ◉ tracing paper
- ◉ colored felt

The Template

Use this template to make the body of the puppet.

How to Use the Template

1 Place tracing paper over the template. Trace around the outline.

2 Cut out the shape on the tracing paper.

You will use this template each time you make a finger puppet.

puppet body template

Making Freddie Frog

To make Freddie Frog, you will need green, red, black, and white felt.

1 Fold over a piece of green felt. Lay your tracing paper body template on top. Using the black felt pen, draw around the shape.

2 Cut out the shape so you have two pieces that are the same. You now have the body for your frog puppet.

3 Fold over another piece of green felt. Draw front and back legs and cut out the shapes so you have four legs.

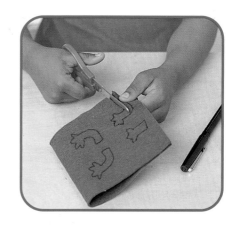

Freddie Frog Takes Shape

4 Fold over a piece of black felt. Using the white color pencil, draw a small circle. Now cut out the circle so you have two black eyes.

5 Fold over a piece of white felt. Using the felt pen, draw a larger circle. Now cut out the circle so you have two white eyes.

6 Using the felt pen, draw a mouth shape on a piece of red felt. Cut it out.

You now have materials for two pairs of legs, two eyes and a mouth. You can start putting your frog puppet together!

Finishing Freddie Frog

7 Arrange the frog arms on one of the body pieces. Glue them into place.

8 Arrange the frog legs on the other body piece. Glue them into place.

9 Glue around the curved edge of one of the body pieces, leaving the bottom edge free. Press the two body pieces together, with the arms and legs in between.

10 Glue the eyes and mouth onto the front of the puppet.

Allow a few hours for the glue to dry and then try out your frog puppet!

Clean up!

Making Polly Panda

To make Polly Panda, you will need black and white felt.

1 Fold over a piece of white felt. Lay your tracing paper body template on top. Using a black felt pen, draw around the shape.

2 Cut out the shape so you have two pieces that are the same. You now have the body for your panda puppet.

3 Fold over a piece of black felt. Draw front and back legs, using the white color pencil. Cut out the shapes so you have four legs.

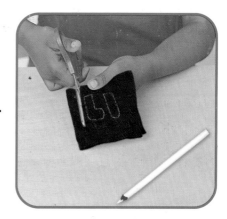

Polly Panda Takes Shape

4 Fold over a piece of black felt. Using the white color pencil, draw a circle. Now cut out the circle so you have two black eyes.

5 Fold over a piece of white felt. Using the felt pen, draw a smaller circle. Now cut out the circle so you have two white eyes.

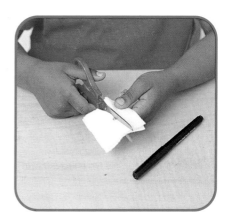

6   Fold over a piece of black felt. Now, using the white color pencil, draw an ear shape on the black felt. Cut out the shape so you have two black ears.

7   Draw nose and mouth shapes on the black felt. Cut out the shapes. You now have a nose and a mouth.

You now have materials for two pairs of legs, two eyes, ears, a nose, and a mouth. You can start putting your panda puppet together!

Finishing Polly Panda

8   Arrange the panda arms and the ears on one of the body pieces. Glue them into place.

9   Arrange the panda legs on the other body piece. Glue them into place.

10   Glue around the curved edge of one of the body pieces, leaving the bottom edge free. Press the two body pieces together, with the arms and legs in between.

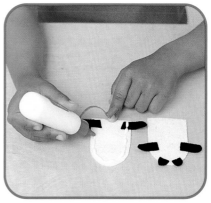

11   Glue the eyes, nose, and mouth onto the front of the puppet.

Allow a few hours for the glue to dry and then try out your panda puppet!

Clean up!

Making Petunia Pig

To make Petunia Pig, you will need pink, black, and white felt.

1 Fold over a piece of pink felt. Lay your tracing paper body template on top. Using a black felt pen, draw around the shape.

2 Cut out the shape so you have two pieces that are the same. You now have the body for your pig puppet.

3 Fold over another piece of pink felt. Draw a back leg. Cut it out so you have two back legs.

Petunia Pig Takes Shape

4 Fold over a piece of black felt. Using the white color pencil, draw a small circle. Now cut out the circle so you have two black eyes.

5 Fold over a piece of pink felt. Using the felt pen, draw an ear shape. Now cut out the shape so you have two pink ears.

6   Using the felt pen, draw
    a curly tail and a round
    nose on a piece of pink felt.
    Cut out the shapes.

7   Fold over a piece of white felt.
    Using the felt pen, draw a
    small circle. Cut out the circle
    so you have two nostrils.

8   Now, using the felt pen, draw
    a small ear shape on the white
    felt. Cut out the shape so you
    have two white inner ears.

You now have materials for a pair of legs, two eyes,
a nose, a tail and two ears. You can start putting your
pig puppet together!

Finishing Petunia Pig

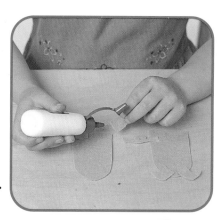

9   Arrange the tail and ears on one of the body pieces. Glue them into place.

10 Arrange the legs on the other body piece. Glue them into place.

11 Glue around the curved edge of one of the body pieces, leaving the bottom edge free. Press the two body pieces together, with the legs, tail, and ears in between.

12 Glue the eyes and pink nose onto the front of the puppet. Then glue the nostrils and inner ears in place.

Allow a few hours for the glue to dry and then try out your pig puppet!

Clean up!

Making Percy Parrot

To make Percy Parrot, you will need red, yellow, green, black, and orange felt.

1 Fold over a piece of red felt. Lay your tracing paper body template on top. Using a black felt pen, draw around the shape.

2 Cut out the shape so you have two pieces that are the same. You now have the body for your parrot puppet.

3 Fold over a piece of yellow felt. Draw a claw shape and cut out the shape so you have two claws.

Percy Parrot Takes Shape

4 Using the felt pen, draw the outline for the parrot's eye shape on a piece of yellow felt. Now cut out the shape.

5 Fold over a piece of black felt. Using the white color pencil, draw a small circle. Now cut out the circle so you have two black eyes.

6 Using the felt pen, draw a beak shape on a piece of orange felt. Now cut out the shape so you have an orange beak.

7 Fold over a piece of yellow felt. Using the felt pen, draw a wing feather shape. Now cut out the shape so you have two yellow feather pieces.

8 Fold over a piece of green felt. Using the felt pen, draw the wing shape. Now cut out the shape so you have two green wings.

You now have materials for a pair of claws, two eyes, the beak, two wings, and the feathers. You can start putting your parrot puppet together!

Finishing Percy Parrot

9   Arrange the parrot wings on one of the body pieces. Glue them into place.

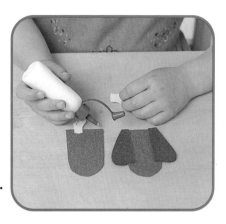

10   Arrange the claws on the other body piece. Glue them into place.

11   Glue around the curved edge of one of the body pieces, leaving the bottom edge free. Press the two body pieces together, with the claws and wings in between.

12   Glue the eye shape and beak onto the front of the puppet. Then glue the black eyes and feather pieces in place.

Allow a few hours for the glue to dry and then try out your parrot puppet!

Clean up!

Ideas for Other Puppets

What other puppets can you make?

Kitty Kat

Peter Pup

Rene Rabbit

Henrietta Hen

Donkey Dave

Leo Lion